STEAM IN EAST ANGLIA
A Colour Portfolio

R. C. Riley

Introduction

The extensive network of lines that served North East London, Essex, Cambridgeshire and East Anglia was developed by a number of companies, the oldest of which was the Eastern Counties Railway, the first portion of which opened in 1839. It started life with the Northern & Eastern Railway as 5ft 0in gauge but soon realised the error of its ways, and its lines were converted to standard gauge in 1844. Other companies quickly followed to exploit the area, notably the Eastern Union Railway, the Norfolk Railway and the East Anglian Railway. By 1854 the Eastern Counties Railway had by degrees taken over the working of these lines, and eight years later the companies were merged to form the Great Eastern Railway. The latter absorbed other companies, such as the Thetford & Watton and Watton & Swaffham Railways. The formation in 1893 of the Midland & Great Northern Joint Railway, bringing together a number of smaller companies, created the only serious rival to the otherwise virtually complete monopoly of the GER in East Anglia.

The original London terminus, Shoreditch, was not only inconveniently located for the City but also unable to cope with increased traffic. The GER obtained an Act in 1865 to build a very costly extension to Liverpool Street, eventually opened in 1874/5.

This was just in time to handle the increased suburban traffic created by extensions to Walthamstow (and thence Chingford) as well as a direct route to Enfield Town, which had been rail-served since 1849. The new terminus was later known as the West Side, after the further development of the East Side station, opened in 1894. Since the Liverpool Street extension inevitably involved the large-scale destruction of workers' dwellings, a condition of the Parliamentary Act was that the GER had to provide cheap workmen's trains to enable the re-housed workers to reach their employment in the metropolis. Initially, special workman's trains were run, the return fare for the 21 miles from Enfield Town being two old pence (or less than a penny in today's coinage). At a later date, Workmen's Fares were available on any train reaching London before 8.0am, and such fares, no longer so cheap, were still available in early BR days. The old Shoreditch terminus, latterly renamed Bishopsgate, served as a goods station until it was destroyed by fire in 1964.

The Eastern Counties Railway had its first locomotive works at Squirrels Heath near Romford, but in 1848 it made the wise decision to move to a more extensive site at Stratford, where an enormous complex of works, engine sheds, carriage sidings and goods yards gradually developed. While the shops at Ilford dealt with electric

Title page: This brings back memories of the West Side train shed as it was, free of overhead wires and with the later Broadgate development far in the future. Hatfield-based Class N7/3 No 69704 heads an empty-stock train while running in after repair at Stratford Works. Darlington-built Class B17/6 'Sandringham' No 61618 *Wynyard Park* stands at the head of the 10.0am parcels train to Ipswich on 4 October 1958. The 'B17s' were introduced in 1928 because of the need to work heavier trains. Some design work was done at Doncaster, but responsibility was handed over to the North British Locomotive Co, which built only the first 10 engines. By 1935 nearly 50, mostly named after country estates, were at work on GE lines. Later engines were named after football clubs, and after work on the GC section all were allocated to GE lines by 1949. Rough riders, the last survived until 1960. *R. C. Riley*

First published 2002

ISBN 0 7110 2892 3

Published by Ian Allan Publishing

an imprint of Ian Allan Publishing Ltd, Hersham, Surrey KT12 4RG.
Printed by Ian Allan Printing Ltd, Hersham, Surrey KT12 4RG.

Code: 0206/B2

locomotives and EMUs, Stratford was home to the diesels until recent years. The site is now considered as a future station on the Channel Tunnel Rail Link.

The GER served such important places as Cambridge, Peterborough, Colchester, Ipswich and Norwich, while it also reached Lincoln and Doncaster by means of the GN & GE Joint line, with running powers to York. In addition it served several ports and holiday resorts on the Essex, Suffolk and Norfolk coasts. It had many rural branch lines and much agricultural traffic, but, with the increased use of road vehicles after World War 1, some of these lost their traffic in LNER days — a process that gained impetus in BR days even before publication of the Beeching Report. The GER also had shipping interests and was a pioneer in the use of motor omnibuses, some of which were built at Stratford.

In early BR days, GER lines were designated 'The Great Eastern Line', and the photographs in this book all date from that era. Under privatisation the line is divided into Great Eastern, Anglia and West Anglia & Great Northern. It is widely expected that, on expiry of the present franchises, the former GER will be combined once again under single ownership.

Acknowledgements
Acknowledgements are due to fellow members of the Great Eastern Railway Society, although any mistakes are mine alone. Membership of the GERS — thoroughly recommended — can be made by application to J. R. Tant, 9 Clare Road, Leytonstone, London E11 1JU. Thanks also to Peter Waller and his colleagues at Ian Allan Publishing Ltd and to my wife, Christine.

Liverpool Street, West Side, 11 May 1957, with Class B17/6 No 61622 *Alnwick Castle* on the 3.33pm to Yarmouth South Town, when that resort had through services from London and before the East Suffolk line was threatened with closure. The line as far as Lowestoft was reprieved, but Yarmouth South Town closed in 1970. Beside it can be seen the famous station pilots — Class N7/4 No 69614, West Side pilot 1956-60, and Class J69 0-6-0T No 68619, East Side pilot 1948-61. No 68633 of the latter class survives at the NRM as GER No 87, a worthy contender for preservation, as before the advent of the 'N7s' they bore the brunt of the intensive services on the Enfield Town and Chingford lines, known as the 'Jazz Trains'. *R. C. Riley*

Above: When it first became East Side pilot in 1948, No 68619 was painted in LNER green livery, which it carried until 1953 when it was painted unlined black, to be lined out four years later. Finally, in September 1959, it emerged in GER blue, complete with GER coat of arms. It was recorded on 2 October 1959 attaching a 1913-built GER dining car to a Newmarket Race Special. *R. C. Riley*

Right: Thompson's general-purpose Class B1 4-6-0s proved a valuable addition to GE-line locomotive stock, and indeed until the arrival of the 'Britannia' 4-6-2s they became the principal main-line passenger engines. No fewer than 410 engines of the 'B1' class were built between 1942 and 1952, mainly by outside contractors. No 61311 was recorded at Liverpool Street on 11 May 1957 on the 5.36pm Clacton train. This was from the East Side of the station built in 1894 and adding eight platforms to the original 10 of the West Side station. The line to Shenfield had been electrified in 1949, and this was extended to Southend Victoria at the end of December 1956. The 'Southend' EMU, later No 126 of Class 307, was newly into traffic for the Southend extension. *R. C. Riley*

Left: Introduction of the 'Britannia' 4-6-2s in 1951 enabled considerable accelerations to take place, with hourly fast trains between London and Norwich. At one time 22 of the 55 members of the class were to be found on GE lines. No 70012 *John of Gaunt* was at the head of the down 'Broadsman', the 3.30pm Liverpool Street–Norwich, on 2 May 1958. In that year, owing to difficulties at Stratford, maintenance of the class was taken over by Norwich, and the full GE-line allocation was transferred there the following year until introduction of main-line diesels displaced them two years later. *R. C. Riley*

Above: Liverpool Street was probably best known for its intensive steam suburban service. Class N7 0-6-2T No 69604 of the 1921 Stratford-built batch was approaching the terminus on a train from Chingford on 4 October 1958 with two Gresley 'Quint-Arts' (five-coach articulated sets). Allocated to Wood Street, Walthamstow, this engine was kept specially clean and is unusual in that these engines normally ran chimney-first from Liverpool Street as they faced the climb to Bethnal Green. Within days the engine was turned to the correct position. *R. C. Riley*

Below: When Class N7 No 69614 was groomed for pilot duties it stirred the Enfield Town men to action, and their engines very soon became equally immaculate. No 69658 heads an Enfield Town train at Bethnal Green, which still then retained the once-familiar GER platform canopies. The white shedplate is distinctly unusual. Although the locomotive was officially allocated to Stratford, full servicing and light repair facilities were available to those engines outstationed at Enfield and Walthamstow. These lines were electrified in 1960 on the 25kV system, to which the existing electrified lines were also converted. *K. W. Wightman*

Right: The last engine built at Stratford Works was Class N7 0-6-2T No 8011 in the first LNER series, later BR No 69621. Stratford built 22 of these very useful engines, and building elsewhere eventually brought the class total to 134. No 69621 was recorded at Palace Gates, having arrived from North Woolwich, in September 1962. This engine was privately preserved by the late Dr R. F. Youell and its home base is the East Anglian Railway Museum at Chappel. *R. Hobbs*

Left: The remarkable 'J15' class 0-6-0s numbered 289 locomotives built between 1883 and 1913. The type had a high route availability, and 127 of them survived to be taken over by BR; No 65361, fitted with steam brake only, was the oldest survivor, built in 1889 and withdrawn in September 1962, the end of steam on GE lines. Also withdrawn at this time was No 65462 of 1912, one of the last 40 engines, which had Westinghouse train brakes and vacuum ejectors. This engine is preserved on the North Norfolk Railway at Sheringham. No 65361 was recorded at Stratford on 7 May 1961. *R. C. Riley*

Above: There were 35 of the 'J18'/'J19' class 0-6-0 goods engines built between 1912 and 1920 — the first GER goods engines to have superheated boilers of the type fitted to the 'Claud Hamilton' 4-4-0s. Between 1935 and 1939 all were rebuilt with boilers of the type fitted to Class D16/3 locomotives. No 64655 was on Stratford shed on 28 May 1958. Among other duties, these engines were to be found on cross-London freights to Hither Green or Feltham. *R. C. Riley*

Completion of electrification of the North East London lines in November 1960 and conversion of the Shenfield and Southend lines from 1,500V dc to 25kV ac was not accomplished without major problems, alleged by BR to be the fault of contractors' equipment. Serious electrical faults caused the withdrawal of both new and converted EMUs, and these were replaced by units from the LT&S line and from as far afield as Crewe. In this study on 7 May 1961 Driving Trailer No E75078 from Shenfield-line EMU No 231 is being shunted into the Engine Repair Shop at Stratford by Class J69 0-6-0T No 68549. *R. C. Riley*

A. J. Hill designed a class of five powerful 0-4-0Ts for shunting yards in the London area. Built between 1913 and 1921, they eventually formed Class Y4. The last of the class, GER No 210 of 1921, was exclusively used shunting the Old Works at Stratford — a function it performed until the works' closure in 1963. Latterly it was numbered 33 in Departmental stock, and in 1949 was fitted with a Class N7-pattern chimney. *R. C. Riley*

Above: Running repairs at Stratford shed were carried out in a two-road shed free of the smoke that always filled the main sheds. It was apparent that this always dealt with a high proportion of GER engines. When recorded on 7 May 1961 it contained five 0-6-0s of Classes J15/J19/J20, two 'N7' 0-6-2Ts, three 'J68'/'J69' class 0-6-0Ts and a 'B1' 4-6-0. *R. C. Riley*

Right: It was not until 1938 that Gresley's powerful Class K3 2-6-0s were allowed to work south of March on the GE section, following major bridge renewals. They were used largely on heavy-freight work to and from Whitemoor Marshalling Yard, but notably at weekends they would appear on main-line passenger work. No 61801 was recorded approaching Stratford with a down relief express to Ipswich. *K. W. Wightman*

Left: Thompson's Class L1 2-6-4Ts were less successful than the 'B1s' and suffered from axlebox and motion wear, leading to a clanking that enabled them to be identified in the distance without seeing them. The 'L1s' had 5ft 2in coupled wheels — 4in larger than those of the 'N7s'. Originally intended in the GE London area for trains to Bishops Stortford or Hertford East, they latterly replaced the 'N7s' on the North Woolwich–Palace Gates service, on which No 67729 was recorded at West Green in September 1962. *Roy Hobbs*

Above: In postwar years 'Claud Hamilton' class 4-4-0s were only rarely to be seen in the London area. These two 'D16/3s', Nos 62580 and 62556, were recorded on an up perishables train near Lea Bridge. The name *Claud Hamilton* was given to the first engine of the class, built in 1900. Lord Claud Hamilton was Chairman of GER from 1893 and was in office until the 1923 railway Grouping. The engine, latterly LNER No 2500, was withdrawn in 1947, although in rebuilt 'D16/3' form, and its name was transferred to No 2546. *K. W. Wightman*

Above: The attractive branch from Epping to Ongar opened in 1865 when the existing line from Loughton was extended thus far. Residential traffic quickly developed, and there were through trains from Epping to Liverpool Street. Before World War 2 some thought had been given to the extension of the Central Line tube into North East London, and by degrees this was achieved as far as Epping in 1949. It was not then considered justifiable to extend to Ongar, and the branch was worked by push-pull trains, mainly with GER 2-4-2Ts, of which type Class F5 No 67193 was noted in a rural part of Epping Forest. *K. W. Wightman*

Right: The Epping–Ongar line was eventually electrified in 1957. Class F5 2-4-2T No 67218 was recorded at Ongar on 18 May 1957. The electrification was not a success in attracting passengers, and, after trials with peak-time-only trains, the branch was closed in 1994. The line is thought to be a suitable candidate for preservation, but some controversy affects the scheme at present. *R. C. Riley*

Left: Awaiting scrap at Stratford, Class D16/3 4-4-0 No 62561 bears a Melton Constable shedplate, while the tender is fitted with a tablet catcher as used on single lines of the former M&GN Joint lines. *R. C. Riley*

Right and below right: A sad sight at the end of steam at Stratford shed on 8 September 1962. From this date the nearest steam allocation on the GE line was at March. *Roy Hobbs*

Above: Marks Tey station looking up towards London. The main line as far as Colchester was opened in 1843 and the Stour Valley line to Sudbury was opened six years later. It is the Sudbury branch that curves round to the right. This was single track with passing loops at some stations. *G. W. Powell*

Right: Class E4 2-4-0 No 62792 stands at Marks Tey with a Cambridge–Colchester train on 9 June 1956; this was to be the engine's last day in service, and it performed very well. The Cambridge–Colchester trains were largely worked by 'E4' 2-4-0s, 'J15' 0-6-0s and 'D16/3' 4-4-0s, but as their numbers diminished so larger engines appeared. *R. C. Riley*

Above: Having arrived on the branch from Bury St Edmunds, Class J15 0-6-0 No 65474 stands at Long Melford beside the Maltings. Opened in 1895, this branch closed to passenger traffic in 1961, freight being handled for another four years. *G. W. Powell*

Right: Class J15 0-6-0 No 65405 stands at Long Melford with the 11.36am Colchester–Cambridge train, 9 June 1956. The extension of the Stour Valley line from Sudbury to Shelford was opened in 1865 and was to close 102 years later, having latterly been served by DMUs. No 65405 was one of five 'J15s' fitted with tender cab and side window for use on the Colne Valley line, which lacked turntable provision. *R. C. Riley*

Above: It was clear that the original terminus at Sudbury was built in such a position as to thwart any future extension, hence the sharp curve of the later 1865 station. The former survived as a goods station until the 1950s. The surviving DMU service to/from Colchester uses a much-truncated portion of platform. In steam days an engine was stabled here overnight. *G. W. Powell*

Right: With the opening of the extension to Shelford, new platforms on a very sharp curve were brought into use. This was the view looking towards Marks Tey. The location also features on the front cover. *G. W. Powell*

Above: The Framlingham branch was an early closure. The line from Wickham Market, opened in 1859, closed to passengers in 1952, although there was adequate freight traffic for it to remain open for freight until 1965. Class J15 0-6-0 No 65389 was recorded at Marlesford on 3 May l958, on the pick-up goods from Ipswich; the train would serve the freight-only branch to Snape Maltings before returning whence it had come. *R. C. Riley*

Right: On the same day, No 65389 crosses the rather flimsy bridge at Snape on its return journey to Ipswich. Opened in 1859, the branch was closed in March 1960. The East Suffolk line, from which these two branches diverged, was also threatened with closure, but local objections saved it, and it is now worked on a simplified basis. The goods agent's house survives at Snape Maltings. *R. C. Riley*

Left: Working a freight train from Whitemoor via the Stour Valley line, Class J20 0-6-0 No 64692 was recorded on the main line just north of Marks Tey. The 25 engines of Class J20 were the most powerful 0-6-0s in Britain until the wartime appearance of Bulleid's 'Q1' 0-6-0s on the Southern Railway. Built from 1920 to 1922, the class became extinct (along with other GER survivors) in 1962. *G. W. Powell*

Below: There were 90 engines of what became LNER Class J17, although one was an early casualty of war, No 8200 being destroyed by a V2 rocket at Channelsea in 1944. All were originally built with steam brake only and were concentrated at March and Peterborough to handle the heavy coal traffic. Replaced by 2-8-0s in LNER days, some engines were fitted with vacuum ejectors after 1942 for work on the M&GN section. Subsequently they became more widely distributed, and No 65578 was recorded at Bentley on the Hadleigh branch goods. No 65567 survives at the NRM in LNER livery as No 8217. *G. W. Powell*

Above: Since many of the first 40 Thompson 'L1s' were used on GE lines, they were fitted with Westinghouse brakes. A member of the first batch, No 67708, was recorded at Westerfield Junction with a Felixstowe train, the fireman having taken the single-line staff. This was the only branch line off the East Suffolk line to survive. *R. C. Riley*

Right: The GER had some 2-4-0 express engines (its Class T19) but needed some smaller 2-4-0s suitable for cross-country and branch-line work. Thus was born the well-remembered 'E4' class, comprising 100 engines built from 1891 to 1902, 18 of which survived to be taken over by British Railways. Remarkably, the maximum axle loading was on the leading wheels, and this made them slightly more restricted than the 'J15s'. This only seemed to affect their use on the Colne Valley & Halstead line, however, and was not significant. The last survivor, No 62785, was withdrawn in 1959 and as GER No 490 is preserved as part of the Bressingham 'Steam Experience', Norfolk. It was recorded working on the Mildenhall branch at the terminus on 4 May 1958. *R. C. Riley*

A glimpse of part of the very long platform at Cambridge on 26 April 1958, as 'E4' 2-4-0 No 62785 waits to work a Cambridge University Railway Club engine-driving and firing special on the Stour Valley line between Linton and Bartlow. Ex-GER coach No E62445E is of interest in showing the retractable steps used at halt platforms. *R. C. Riley*

Class J15 0-6-0 No 65477 was busily employed as south end station pilot at Cambridge on 23 June 1958. This was one of the last 40 members of the class, fitted with Westinghouse brake and vacuum ejector. It was this batch that could frequently be seen on country-branch passenger trains, although they were proved to be capable of hauling quite heavy trains on the main line. *R. C. Riley*

Left: Contrary to what has been published elsewhere, the only 'E4' to receive full lining-out was No 62790, seen at Marks Tey on 3 June 1950. The remainder of the class were painted unlined black in BR days, as was No 62790 on its next works visit. *G. W. Powell*

Above: The interesting feature of Class E4 No 62784, seen at Marks Tey on the Stour Valley line on 31 July 1954, was the fact that it was the last GER engine with a so-called 'watercart' tender. These had been attached to older engines equipped for oil burning, and originally carried two cylindrical oil tanks. When modified to carry coal, these adapted tenders were found on Class D13 4-4-0s (rebuilt from GER Class T19 2-4-0s) and Class E4 2-4-0s. The last one was attached to No 62784 from August 1953 until withdrawal of this engine in May 1955. *G. W. Powell*

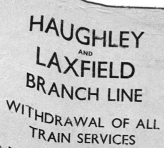

Opposite: The Mid-Suffolk Light Railway was one of a few such lines authorised under the 1896 Light Railways Act. Its grandiose plans never came to fruition, and the only line built was from Haughley to Laxfield, opened in 1904. Serving a sparsely populated area, it was an early candidate for closure, and the last train ran on 26 July 1952. A 'J15' 0-6-0 was outstationed at Laxfield — usually No 65447, which was kept immaculate by the local crews and was recorded there on 22 July 1952. *G. W. Powell*

Below: Although taken over by the LNER in 1923, the MSLR retained an independent station at Haughley until November 1939, when layout changes giving direct access were made in anticipation of increased traffic resulting from World War 2. A bay was then provided on the up platform, and No 65447 was recorded there, having just arrived from Laxfield, on 22 July 1952. Three of the line's station buildings survive — one at Brockford (now a museum to the MSLR) and two more at Mangapps Farm Railway Museum, Burnham-on-Crouch. *G. W. Powell*

Left: The seven-mile branch from Bentley to Hadleigh opened in 1847 as the result of local endeavours but was taken over by the Eastern Union Railway in 1848. Bentley station was a dull wooden building, but the stations on the branch were brick-built in Italianate style. This view shows Capel station, where, prior to rebuilding on a new formation, the level crossing protected what was then the A12 trunk road between Colchester and Ipswich. Recorded on 9 June 1956, the line had lost its passenger traffic in 1932. *G. W. Powell*

Above: As a listed building, Hadleigh station, seen in 1956, remained unused for many years, but is now a private dwelling set in the midst of a new housing estate. Goods traffic continued until 1965, with the train crew operating the level crossings *en route*. *G. W. Powell*

Below: At a time when the East Suffolk line was still thriving, with through trains to/from London, Class B17/6 'Sandringham' 4-6-0s No 61665 *Leicester City* and No 61664 *Liverpool* head an up express near Wickham Market on Sunday 4 May 1958. The double-heading was required to provide motive power for an additional down train from Ipswich. *R. C. Riley*

Right: Class B17/6 4-6-0 No 61646 *Gilwell Park* stands at March shed on 23 June 1958. With an allocation of 165 engines, including 10 of the 'Sandringhams', in the 1950s this was the second-largest (after Stratford) motive power depot on GE lines. *R. C. Riley*

Below: Thompson's Class B1 4-6-0s eventually numbered 410 engines. Introduced in wartime, the first 10 engines were built at Darlington from 1942 to 1944. The first 20 of the production series went to GE sheds — Nos 1040-52 to Norwich and Nos 1053-9 to Ipswich — although No 1057 would be destroyed in an accident in dense fog at Witham on 7 March 1950. The first 41 engines numerically were named after species of antelope; No 61001 *Eland*, recorded at Ipswich shed on 22 May 1957, was the second of the class built (as LNER No 8302) and was allocated to the GE section from new. Stratford shed had No 61005 *Bongo* on its books and used this as a nickname for the class! *R. C. Riley*

Right: Ten of the Class B17 'Sandringhams' were rebuilt by Thompson with two cylinders and Class B1 boilers. As the 'B17s' were in any case being fitted with Class B1 boilers, the more drastic Class B2 rebuilds showed little advantage, and only 10 were so treated. They shared the criticism of the unrebuilt engines, that they were rough riding. The last 'B2' was withdrawn in 1959, the last of the 'B17s' surviving for another year. Recorded at Linton, No 61616 *Fallodon* was working a Cambridge University Railway Club special. *R. C. Riley*

Above: Rebuilt Class D16/3 'Claud Hamilton' 4-4-0 No 62546 leaves Halesworth for Yarmouth on 6 October 1956. The pioneer engine of the class, No 2500 *Claud Hamilton*, was withdrawn in 1947, its nameplate being transferred to the locomotive pictured, which survived until June 1957. *R. C. Riley*

Right: By now the last survivor of Class D16/3, No 62613 was recorded tender-first on a train to King's Lynn, at Hunstanton on 1 June 1960, the turntable at the latter having been removed in the late 1950s. The locomotive was withdrawn from service four months after the photograph was taken. *R. C. Riley*

Left: The most important of the GER passenger engines built between 1911 and 1920 were the 70 engines of the 'B12' class. A further 10 were built in LNER days by Beyer Peacock in 1928. When Edward Thompson was Assistant Mechanical Engineer at Stratford he rebuilt several GE classes, including 54 of the 'B12s', which were able to carry a heavier axle loading following bridge rebuilding. Even so, they had a high route availability, which enabled members of the class to be loaned to the US Army in World War 2 for the haulage of US Ambulance Trains, mainly on the SR and GWR. By the time it was photographed at Norwich shed, on 31 May 1960, No 61572 was the last survivor; it was withdrawn the following year and fortunately was purchased for preservation on the North Norfolk Railway at Sheringham. *R. C. Riley*

Below: Electrification of the Shenfield–Southend line at the end of 1956 brought about withdrawal of some of Stratford's surviving 'B12/3s', although others went to country sheds to replace 'D16/3s'. No 61553 was withdrawn in August 1958 and was seen at Stratford on 10 August 1958. *R. C. Riley*

Above: BR 'Britannia' class 4-6-2 No 70003 *John Bunyan* leaves Thetford with the RCTS GE Commemorative Railtour, 31 March 1962. Dieselisation of the GE main lines had seen the allocation of these engines shared between March and Immingham by the latter part of 1961, and thereafter they would never be cared for as much as they had been at Norwich shed under the jurisdiction of the late D. W. Harvey. *Roy Hobbs*

Right: A railtour of a totally different type! No 65469 pauses at Ingham on the Bury–Thetford line with a brake-van special, 11 June 1960. At Norwich shed Mr Harvey had cut the top off two 'J15' chimneys and welded on a new top, giving the effect of a stovepipe chimney. The engines chosen were Nos 65469 and 65471; No 65469 retained this chimney until withdrawal. When No 65471 went for scrap its chimney was transferred to No 65462, which survives on the North Norfolk Railway. *R. C. Riley*

Left: Gresley's powerful 'K3' class was introduced in 1920, as GNR Class H4, and 10 had been built for the GNR by 1921. Recently outshopped when recorded at Norwich shed on 31 May 1960, No 61810 was the first of the 'production' batch built at Darlington in 1924. Other than at March, it was several years before they were allowed on GE lines, where in good condition they were very popular. *R. C. Riley*

Below: Peppercorn's 'K1s' were based on Thompson's rebuild of Gresley 'K4' No 3445, 70 engines being built in 1949/50. Of these, 30 were sent originally to March for the coal traffic from the GN&GE Joint line. No 62051 works an up freight through Bishops Stortford on 12 September 1959. Allocation of these engines enabled less popular Class K2 2-6-0s to be transferred away from GE lines. *R. C. Riley*

Left: Class K3 2-6-0 No 61949 heads empty wagons approaching Coke Ovens Junction, Lowestoft, on 22 May 1957. At this time there was a considerable volume of fish traffic. *R. C. Riley*

Above: Always willing to experiment, the LNER tried out a Sentinel vertical-boilered steam locomotive in 1925. The trials were considered successful, and eventually 56 such engines were allocated throughout the system. Numbered 40 in Departmental stock, the former LNER No 63 of 1930, photographed on 22 May 1957, was one of those used from time to time to shunt at the Lowestoft sleeper depot. The one-time LNER No 59 is preserved on the Middleton Railway, Leeds. *R. C. Riley*

Below: The first 'Super Clauds' of Class D16 followed the rebuilding of No 1805 (LNER No 8805) in 1923. A few months later, the last 10 'Claud Hamiltons' — Nos 1780-9 (LNER 8780-9) — were built in this form, and eventually, following further rebuilding, there were 40 'Super Clauds'. Nos 8783 and 8787 attained fame as Royal Engines covering the Royal Family's journeys to and from Sandringham. Upon rebuilding to Class D16/3, the Class D16/2 'Super Clauds' retained the decorative valances over the coupling rods, with one exception: No 8783, damaged in a level crossing accident at Hilgay on 1 June 1939, was rebuilt as Class D16/3 with the cutaway frames, as on rebuilds of the earlier 'D15' engines. The Royal 'Clauds' lost their green paint during the war. In January 1946 No 8783 (later 2614 and eventually BR 62614) was repainted green, followed by No 62618 (previously LNER 2618 and earlier 8787) in October 1949. By April 1952 both were in the lined black livery shared with those engines of Class D16/3 still in service. No 62614 was recorded in green at King's Lynn on 6 July 1950. *G. W. Powell*

Right: From whatever angle they were viewed, the Class D16/3 'Clauds' looked handsome, with decorative valancing. The last survivor, No 62613, was recorded at King's Lynn on 1 June 1960, about to work to Hunstanton, which at one time had its own shed. This locomotive was withdrawn in October 1960, at which time private locomotive preservation had not got underway. *R. C. Riley*

Above: The 1.7pm Lowestoft–Whitemoor van train stands at Kimberley Park, near Wymondham on the mid-Norfolk line, on 31 May 1960. This train was scheduled to leave Norwich at 2.31pm. At Dereham the train reversed, but the engine was turned on the triangle then existing to set off for King's Lynn via Swaffham. This duty was often performed by No 61572, the last surviving Class B12/3, in its last months of service. On arrival at King's Lynn the train reversed and Ivatt 2-6-0 No 43161 took over. *R. C. Riley*

Right: Although the Framlingham branch closed to passenger traffic in 1952, special trains continued to run for the College at the beginning and end of term and at half-term. On this occasion, 2 May 1958, the train consisted of the rear three coaches of the 3.33pm Liverpool Street–Yarmouth. These would normally have formed the 5.20pm to Felixstowe, which was cancelled on that day. The Framlingham platform just accommodated the engine and three coaches. Once unloaded, the coaches were propelled into the yard by 'B12/3' No 61561, which then ran round and returned to Ipswich tender-first with the empty stock. Remarkably, the Liverpool Street booking office provided a printed ticket to Framlingham. The College specials ceased to run after this date. *R. C. Riley*

The Gresley Class J39 0-6-0s were introduced in 1926, and by 1941 there were 289 in service throughout the LNER system. Stratford had the largest share of the 74 engines allocated to the GE section, of which 20 had Westinghouse brakes. Notably in prewar days these locomotives were used, perhaps unsuitably, on relief trains to Clacton or Southend. At Ipswich shed on 22 May 1957, No 64800 was being prepared to work a freight to Felixstowe. *R. C. Riley*

After World War 1 the LNER purchased 273 of the Great Central Railway 2-8-0s from the Ministry of Munitions. When Thompson succeeded Gresley as CME he decided to modernise these engines with boiler and cylinders of the type used on the 'B1s' and Walschaerts valve gear. They were highly successful in this form, and between 1944 and 1949 there were 58 engines rebuilt thus. Some were allocated to March, where they found use on Whitemoor–Temple Mills freights, also appearing elsewhere on the GE section from time to time. Originally built in 1918, No 63650 was rebuilt in 1945 and ran for another 20 years. It is pictured at Stratford shed on 7 May 1961. *R. C. Riley*

Left: Continuing the theme of engines used on Whitemoor–Temple Mills freight trains, Class K1 2-6-0 No 62040 was recorded at Stratford on 7 May 1961. If these March-allocated engines found themselves at Stratford over a weekend they could well be pressed into service on relief passenger trains. *R. C. Riley*

Below: Again, it was from March shed that these ex-War Department Austerity locomotives worked, mainly to London but also to Lowestoft and Ipswich. No 90559 (ex-WD No 77095), built at Vulcan Foundry in 1943, was recorded at Stratford on 7 May 1961. Interestingly this engine was in Stratford Works when only a year old, whereupon the Ministry Inspector condemned the boiler, a replacement being provided by Vulcan Foundry. Other, less drastic cases occurred, and the standard of steel supplied in wartime may have been to blame. *R. C. Riley*

Below: Despite their antique appearance, the Class J15 0-6-0s were powerful engines, the 'maids of all work' on GE lines. No 65445, one of the final batch, with Westinghouse brakes, stands at Harwich on 13 June 1960. Built in 1899, it survived until nearly the end of steam on GE lines, in August 1962. *R. W. Smith*

Right: At the 1923 Grouping the GER provided 10 engines of LNER Class J18 and 25 engines of Class J19, all built between 1912 and 1920. All were rebuilt in the 1930s with the boiler designed for Class D16/3 locomotives. In this form Class J19/2 0-6-0 No 64646 was observed at Takeley with a Railway Club brake-van special on the freight-only Bishops Stortford–Braintree line. The line lost its passenger traffic in 1952, and 20 years later the last freight service was withdrawn. *R. C. Riley*

Left: The handsome 0-6-0s built from 1920 to 1922 which became LNER Class J20 were the most powerful engines of their type, not only on the GER but in the whole country. Only in 1942, when Bulleid's 'Q1' 0-6-0s first emerged from works, were they beaten into second place. They originally had the same type of boiler as the '1500' class ('B12') 4-6-0s in unrebuilt form. This was redesigned by Thompson with a round-topped firebox, but otherwise the 'J20s' remained as built. As has been seen already, they put in some time on the Whitemoor–Temple Mills coal trains, but as they were replaced by 2-8-0s they appeared more generally. In 1959 Nos 64678/9 were sent to Parkeston to shunt wagons on and off the train ferries. No 64678 was so recorded on 19 June 1960. *R. W. Smith*

Above right: The Brightlingsea branch was five miles long, running from Wivenhoe off the Clacton branch alongside the River Colne. The disastrous East Coast floods of January 1953 washed out three miles of the line, and it was only reopened in December 1953 because local protest forced BR to do so. However, it did not survive the Beeching Report and closed in June 1964. Class J69 0-6-0 No 68573 was in charge of the branch goods train on 13 June 1960. *R. W. Smith*

Right: With the construction of Class N7 0-6-2Ts in early LNER days, a number of 'J69' 0-6-0Ts were displaced, and these were such useful shunting engines that 20 were sent to Scotland, while others could be found around the system. Among the Scottish batch was No 68635, built in 1904, which spent 14 years as station pilot at Perth. It was recorded at Peterborough's New England shed on 31 May 1958. Unlike the GE-based engines it retained a low cab roof and stovepipe chimney. *R. C. Riley*

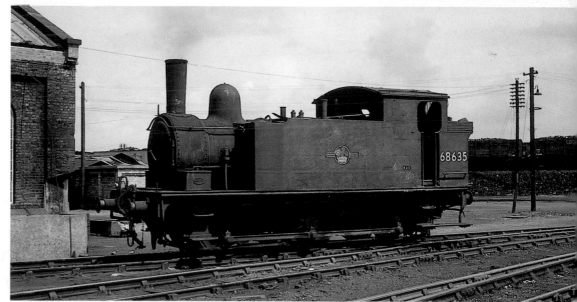

The charming branch line which ran from Long Melford (on the Stour Valley line) to Bury St Edmunds had some pleasant and well-tended stations. Not least among these was Welnetham, which retained its original GER-style blue enamel nameplate, now to be found in the NRM. This was the first of the Stour Valley line's branches to lose its passenger traffic, in 1961. *G. W. Powell*

With only four trains per day each way, the station staff on the Long Melford–Bury St Edmunds line were hardly overstretched and as at Cockfield they had plenty of time to devote to the station gardens.
G. W. Powell

Below: The cathedral city of Ely was reached in 1845; two years later, lines to King's Lynn and Peterborough via March were opened, followed by a line to Newmarket, making Ely a busy junction. Class D16/3 4-4-0 No 62522 approaches with the 2.3pm from King's Lynn via March on 26 April 1958. The GER favoured high signal posts in some locations, and this Saxby & Farmer example had the splitting distant signals for Ely North Junction; the arms refer to the lines to Norwich, King's Lynn and March, in order of importance. It survived until 1963. *R. C. Riley*

Right: Following a collision in fog at Stratford Western Junction between a Woolwich train and a light engine in 1878, the decision was taken to introduce fogging indicators, the miniature arms of which repeated the aspects of the main signals and equally had fail-safe counter balances, as seen at Ely North Junction on 26 April 1958. Note the lever for placing detonators on the track. *R. C. Riley*

Having arrived at King's Lynn on 21 May 1957, Class D16/3 4-4-0 No 62518 stands on shed ready to return to March. Behind it, Class J19/2 0-6-0 No 64669 was acting as carriage pilot at what was then a busy station. Note that the oldest 'Clauds' rebuilt to Class D16/3 lost their decorative valances. *R. C. Riley*

Below: The delightful Kelvedon & Tollesbury line was built under the 1896 Light Railways Act, there being much fruit traffic, notably at Tiptree, to justify the line's existence. In 1928, with closure of the Wisbech & Upwell Tramway, the latter's coaches were transferred to the line. However, main-line passengers had to re-book at Kelvedon. These coaches were among the last gas-lit stock on BR. The body of one survives at the Rutland Railway Museum — a reminder of the *Titfield Thunderbolt* film. Class J67 No 68616 was in charge on 31 July 1950. *G. W. Powell*

Right: The GER introduced tram engines of both four- and six-wheeled type for use on lines on or near the public highway, notably the docks at Ipswich and Yarmouth, but best remembered were those working the Wisbech & Upwell Tramway. These engines had to comply with Board of Trade regulations, being equipped with cowcatchers, skirtings over the wheels, warning bells and a speed governor restricting them to 8mph. There were eight four-wheeled tram engines (Class Y6) and 12 six-wheelers (Class J70). After closure of the Wisbech & Upwell Tramway to passenger traffic at the end of 1927, two engines sufficed to work the line, except during busier periods of the fruit season. Class J70 0-6-0T No 68223 is pictured on Wisbech shed. *R. E. Vincent/ Steam & Sail*

Below: A refugee from the London suburban area, Class F5 2-4-2T No 67229 was occupied on both freight and carriage shunting at Lowestoft Coke Ovens Junction on 22 May 1957. *R. C. Riley*

Right: On the turntable at King's Lynn shed, Class D16/3 4-4-0 No 62610, having arrived from Ely, was preparing to return there on 23 June 1958. Although one of the later engines built, it was not chosen for 'D16/2' rebuilding and so lost its decorative valances on eventual rebuilding to Class D16/3. *R. C. Riley*

Left: Class J15 0-6-0 No 65462 was sold from Norwich shed to the North Norfolk Railway on withdrawal in September 1962, having survived until the end of steam on GE lines. On its first return to steam it was restored in GER grey livery, with its original GER number (564) and still carrying the David Harvey 'stovepipe'! It has since run in LNER livery but is currently undergoing heavy repair. The late David Harvey looks on. *R. C. Riley*

Above: The first and only meeting of two well-respected GER enthusiasts, sadly no longer with us. Dr Ian C. Allen was discussing matters GER with the Rev Teddy Boston at Stoke Ferry station, 8 May 1964. The branch from Denver to Stoke Ferry opened in 1882 and, like the Wisbech & Upwell line, used tramway-style coaches; the service ran to and from Downham Market. Passenger traffic ceased in 1930, but Stoke Ferry remained open to general freight traffic until 1965. *R. C. Riley*

Above: Abbey station, on the Stoke Ferry branch, really served the village of West Dereham but took its name from a monastic ruin so as to avoid confusion with Dereham, some 15 miles away. This was the last station before the Wissington Railway was reached, and this provided much traffic to the main line until eventual closure in 1981. The British Sugar Corporation had established an important factory served by the Wissington Railway, which, being on private land, had been built without Act of Parliament. Abbey station was demolished by 1980. Prior to this, the local engines, otherwise confined to the Exchange Sidings, could visit only on Sundays; *Newcastle*, a Manning

Wardle 0-6-0ST of 1901, was recorded on 27 November 1964. This locomotive is now privately preserved. *R. C. Riley*

Right: Wissington, a Hudswell Clarke 0-6-0ST which was new to the railway in 1938, stands at the end of the Exchange Sidings on 8 May 1964. These tracks and those on the one-time railway into the Fens were not visited by the weed-control train. Apart from those on preserved lines, *Wissington* would be the last operational steam engine in Norfolk, its last steaming being in 1972 to help cover for a failed diesel. It is now preserved on the North Norfolk Railway. *R. C. Riley*

Index of Locations

Abbey & West Dereham	78, 79	Long Melford	24, 25
Bentley	31	Lowestoft	54, 55, 74
Bishops Stortford	53	March	43
Brightlingsea	67	Marks Tey	22, 23, 30, 36, 37
Cambridge	34, 35	Marlesford	28
Capel	40	Mildenhall	33
Cockfield	69	New England, Peterborough	67
Ely	70	Norwich	48, 52
Enfield Town	8	Ongar	19
Epping Forest	18	Palace Gates, Wood Green	9
Framlingham	59	Parkeston Quay	66
Hadleigh (Suffolk)	41	Sheringham	76
Halesworth	46	Snape	29
Harwich	64	Stoke Ferry	77
Haughley	39	Stratford	10, 11, 12, 13, 14, 15, 20, 21, 49, 61, 62, 63
Hunstanton	47		
Ingham	51	Sudbury	Front cover, 26, 27
Ipswich	44, 60	Takeley	65
King's Lynn	56, 57, 71, 75	Thetford	50
Kimberley Park	58	Tiptree	72
Laxfield	38	Weltnetham	68
Lea Bridge	17	West Green	16
Linton	45	Westerfield Junction	32
London (Liverpool Street)	Back cover, 1, 3, 4, 5, 6, 7	Wickham Market	42
		Wisbech	73

Front cover: With the need before World War 2 to run regular Royal Trains to and from Wolferton on the Hunstanton branch, two rebuilt Class D16/3 4-4-0s were maintained as Royal Engines — Nos 8783 and 8787, later 2614 and 2618 after the LNER's 1946 renumbering scheme. By the time of this photograph, Cambridge was using Class B2 No 61671 *Royal Sovereign* as Royal Engine and No 62618 became a 'common user' allotted to any suitable duty. Only superficially cleaned, it was recorded at Sudbury on the 10.5am through train to Clacton on 25 July 1956. *G. W. Powell*

Back cover: Immaculately turned out from Norwich shed, 'Britannia' No 70041 *Sir John Moore* was recorded at Liverpool Street on 26 October 1959, about to work the 9.30am departure to Norwich. By this time the first main-line diesels had arrived on GE lines, and steam traction was to last only another three years. *R. C. Riley*